THIS BOOK GETS AROUND

RETURN TO SENDER
212

**PASS IT OUT
GET IT BACK
BE SURPRISED**
RULES INSIDE

BOOK BELONGS TO

simply for students

YouthMinistry.com/TOGETHER

This Book Gets Around
Pass It Out. Get It Back. Be Surprised.

© 2013 Kurt Johnston

group.com
simplyyouthministry.com

Credits
Author: Kurt Johnston
Executive Developer: Nadim Najm
Chief Creative Officer: Joani Schultz
Editor: Rob Cunningham
Cover Art and Production: Veronica Preston

ISBN 978-1-4707-0658-6

10 9 8 7 6 5 4 3   20 19 18 17 16 15 14 13

Printed in the United States of America.

CONTENTS

PAGES 26-27: _____

PAGES 28-29: _____

PAGES 30-31: _____

PAGES 32-33: _____

PAGES 34-35: _____

PAGES 36-37: _____

PAGES 38-39: _____

PAGES 40-41: _____

PAGES 42-43: _____

PAGES 44-45: _____

PAGES 46-47: _____

THIS
BOOK
GETS
AROUND

PAGES 48-49: _____

PAGES 50-51: _____

PAGES 52-53: _____

PAGES 54-55: _____

Back in the day—way back in the day (around 400 B.C.)—the Greek philosopher (*philosopher* is a fancy word for "Smart person who thinks about lots of stuff") Socrates said, *"The unexamined life is not worth living."* That's a pretty bold statement, and if it's true, then we had better start examining ourselves (that's not nearly as awkward as it sounds).

It's amazing how much you can learn about yourself and others when you take the time to ask a few questions. When answered honestly, the right kinds of questions and activities can be a really fun way to learn more about yourself and discover things you never knew about your friends and family.

Here's how *THIS BOOK GETS AROUND* works (it's quite simple, really):

As the owner of this copy of *This Book Gets Around*, you can decide how you want to use it. There are at least THREE fun options!

Option #1 is for you to use this as a personal journal and fill it out yourself. No special instructions needed—just go for it! Keep in mind, you'll probably have quite a few empty pages, since the same questions are asked over and over a few different times.

Option #2 is for you to give it to somebody, asking that person to fill out one of the two-page spreads, write their name on the Contents page for the pages they completed, and then return it to you when finished. You then pick the next person to give the book to. By doing it this way, you control exactly who gets to fill out the pages of the book.

Option #3 is for you to give it to somebody, asking that person to fill out one of the two-page spreads and to then pass it on to somebody else, who passes it on to somebody else, and so on until the book is completely full. The journal eventually gets back to you, and you get the experience of discovering who filled out the pages. Fun stuff.

To make it easy, we have included separate instruction pages for Option #2 and Option #3. If you choose to pass the journal around, simply tear out this intro page PLUS the instruction page you DON'T want, and give the journal to your first friend. That person will read the instructions and, after filling out a two-page spread, either give it back to you or pass it along to someone else.

How *This Book Gets Around* Works:

It's quite simple, really. *This Book Gets Around* is a fun way for friends to learn a little more about each other! Just fill out the first available two-page spread (there may be lots of pages left or only a few, depending on how much it has traveled before coming to you), write your name on the Contents page for the pages you completed, and return the book to the person who gave it to you—which should be the person who owns the journal, and their name is probably written on the cover.

That's it! You have just helped your friend's effort to get the entire book filled up.

IMPORTANT NOTE: Remember, this book is *not* private! What you write on the pages you fill out will be read by everybody else who gets their hands on this journal. So don't write stuff you don't want others to see, and don't share stuff about yourself you don't want others to know. If there is a question you don't want to answer or an activity you don't want to participate in, just leave it blank. No biggie.

How *This Book Gets Around* Works:

It's quite simple, really. *This Book Gets Around* is a fun way for friends to learn a little more about each other! Just fill out the first available two-page spread (there may be lots of pages left or only a few, depending on how much it has traveled before coming to you), write your name on the Contents page for the pages you completed, and then pass it on to another friend or classmate. They will do the same thing until all the pages are filled up. The final person will return the book to the person who owns it, which should be the person whose name is written on the front.

That's it! You have just helped someone's effort to get the entire book filled up.

RETURN TO SENDER 212

IMPORTANT NOTE: Remember, this book is *not* private! What you write on the pages you fill out will be read by everybody else who gets their hands on this journal. So don't write stuff you don't want others to see, and don't share stuff about yourself you don't want others to know. If there is a question you don't want to answer or an activity you don't want to participate in, just leave it blank. No biggie.

NAME

THIS BOOK GETS AROUND

DON'T FORGET...

...TO WRITE YOUR NAME ON THE CONTENTS PAGE AT THE BEGINNING OF TH BOOK, NEXT TO THE NUMBERS OF THE PAGES BELOW.

FAVORITE ITEM OF CLOTHING:

FAVORITE HOBBY:

WHEN FEELING SAD, WHAT CHEERS YOU UP?

A FOOD YOU'VE NEVER TRIED, BUT WANT TO:

WHEN YOU HAVE AN HOUR OF FREE TIME, WHAT DO YOU LIKE TO DO?

PICK ONE...AND CIRCLE IT!

- WAKE UP EARLY OR SLEEP IN?
- FOLD YOUR TP OR WAD IT UP?

IF YOU COULD ASK GOD ONE
QUESTION, WHAT WOULD IT BE?

YOU ARE KING OR QUEEN FOR A DAY. WHAT LAW
DO YOU CREATE?

ADVICE YOUR PARENTS GAVE YOU THAT YOU ACTUALLY
LISTENED TO:

A PET YOU WISH YOU HAD:

WHAT IS THE KEY TO HAPPINESS?

WISE WORDS:

THERE ARE NO
SHORTCUTS TO
ANY PLACE
WORTH GOING.

DRAW A PORTRAIT OF
YOURSELF HERE:

NAME

THIS
BOOK
GETS
AROUND

DON'T FORGET...

...TO WRITE YOUR NAME ON THE CONTENTS PAGE AT THE BEGINNING OF TH BOOK, NEXT TO THE NUMBERS OF THE PAGES BELOW.

FAVORITE BAND/SINGER OF ALL TIME:

FAVORITE AFTER-SCHOOL SNACK:

WHAT'S SOMETHING YOU'RE REALLY GOOD AT?

IF YOU COULD ASK GOD ONE QUESTION,
WHAT WOULD IT BE?

IF YOU COULD LIVE ANYWHERE IN THE WORLD,
WHERE WOULD YOU LIVE?

WRITE YOUR
FAVORITE JOKE HERE:

WHAT YOU ARE LIKE ON THE INSIDE MATTERS MORE THAN WHAT YOU LOOK LIKE ON THE OUTSIDE.

MOST EMBARRASSING MOMENT:

WHAT SCARES YOU THE MOST?

WHO HAS HAD THE BIGGEST IMPACT ON YOUR LIFE? IN WHAT WAY?

IF YOUR LIFE WERE MADE INTO A MOVIE, WHAT WOULD THE MOVIE TITLE BE?

WHAT WORLD CAUSE OR ISSUE DO YOU CARE MOST ABOUT?

PICK ONE...AND CIRCLE IT!

- PLAY SPORTS OR READ A BOOK?
- HAVE WORLD'S SQUEAKIEST VOICE OR WORLD'S STINKIEST FEET?

NAME

THIS
BOOK
GETS
AROUND

DON'T FORGET...

...TO WRITE YOUR NAME ON THE CONTENTS PAGE AT THE BEGINNING OF THE BOOK, NEXT TO THE NUMBERS OF THE PAGES BELOW.

FAVORITE MOVIE OF ALL TIME:

FAVORITE RADIO STATION:

SOMETHING THAT MAKES YOU LAUGH:

IF YOU COULD ASK GOD ONE QUESTION, WHAT WOULD IT BE?

IF YOU COULD ONLY EAT ONE TYPE OF FOOD FOR THE REST OF YOUR LIFE, WHAT WOULD IT BE?

DRAW A PICTURE OF YOUR FAVORITE ANIMAL
(USING YOUR OPPOSITE HAND!)

THE MOMENT YOU WERE MOST PROUD
OF YOURSELF:

PHYSICAL FEATURE YOU LIKE MOST ABOUT YOURSELF:

WHAT IS YOUR FAVORITE FAMILY MEMORY OR FAMILY
TRADITION?

IF YOU COULD GO BACK IN TIME,
WHAT EVENT WOULD YOU WANT TO SEE IN REAL LIFE?

WHAT DO YOU THINK ARE THE THREE MOST
IMPORTANT QUALITIES IN A FRIEND?

PICK ONE...AND CIRCLE IT!

- EAT A BOOGER OR EAT A BUG?
- SCARY MOVIES OR FUNNY MOVIES?

11

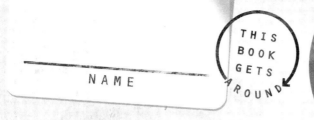

NAME

THIS BOOK GETS AROUND

DON'T FORGET...

...TO WRITE YOUR NAME ON THE CONTENTS PAGE AT THE BEGINNING OF THE BOOK, NEXT TO THE NUMBERS OF THE PAGES BELOW.

FAVORITE BOOK WHEN YOU WERE LITTLE:

FAVORITE SATURDAY ACTIVITY:

IF YOU HAD TO GET A TATTOO, WHAT WOULD IT BE?

IF YOU COULD ASK GOD ONE QUESTION, WHAT WOULD IT BE?

WHAT'S THE BEST VIDEO GAME YOU'VE EVER PLAYED?

PICK ONE...AND CIRCLE IT!

- GET GUM IN YOUR HAIR OR STEP IN DOG POOP WITH BARE FEET?
- GO TO PARIS WITH YOUR FAMILY OR GO CAMPING WITH YOUR FRIENDS?

THINK OUTSIDE THE BOX! USE
AS MUCH SPACE AS YOU WANT
TO DOODLE, DRAW, OR CREATE
SOMETHING FUN ON THIS PAGE!

WHAT'S SOMETHING YOU'RE REALLY GOOD AT?

WHAT DAREDEVIL STUNT WOULD YOU LIKE TO TRY?

WHAT FAMOUS PERSON WOULD YOU LIKE TO TAKE
TO A SCHOOL DANCE?

IF YOU COULD BE AN ANIMAL FOR A WEEK,
WHAT WOULD YOU BE?

IF YOU COULD DO ANYTHING YOU WANTED WITH YOUR
LIFE AND KNEW YOU WOULDN'T FAIL, WHAT WOULD
YOU DO?

WISE WORDS:

LOYALTY AND
KINDNESS ARE TWO
KEYS TO A GREAT
REPUTATION!

NAME

THIS BOOK GETS AROUND

DON'T FORGET...

...TO WRITE YOUR NAME ON THE CONTENTS PAGE AT THE BEGINNING OF THE BOOK, NEXT TO THE NUMBERS OF THE PAGES BELOW.

FAVORITE AND LEAST FAVORITE
SCHOOL SUBJECTS:

FAVORITE APP:

WHAT IS THE BEST CHRISTMAS PRESENT
YOU'VE EVER RECEIVED?

IF YOU COULD ASK GOD ONE QUESTION,
WHAT WOULD IT BE?

YOU ARE 16 AND JUST GOT YOUR DRIVER'S LICENSE—
WHAT CAR ARE YOU DRIVING AND WHERE DO YOU
GO FIRST?

PICK ONE...AND CIRCLE IT!

- PASS GAS UNCONTROLLABLY OR
  HAVE NONSTOP BODY ODOR?

- RUN A MARATHON OR RUN FOR GOVERNOR?

WISE WORDS:

DESCRIBE YOURSELF IN ONE SENTENCE:

IF THERE WERE ONLY ONE TYPE OF CANDY IN THE
WORLD, WHAT SHOULD IT BE?

A PET YOU WISH YOU HAD:

IF THE NEWSPAPER WROTE A FRONT-PAGE ARTICLE
ABOUT YOU, WHAT WOULD THE HEADLINE BE?

WHAT ARE THE THREE MOST IMPORTANT
QUALITIES IN A FRIEND?

WITHOUT LIFTING YOUR
PEN OR PENCIL, DRAW A
MOTORCYCLE

NAME

THIS BOOK GETS AROUND

DON'T FORGET...

...TO WRITE YOUR NAME ON THE CONTENTS PAGE AT THE BEGINNING OF THE BOOK, NEXT TO THE NUMBERS OF THE PAGES BELOW.

FAVORITE WEBSITE:

TOP THREE FAVORITE SONGS:

IMAGINE MAKING A YOUTUBE® VIDEO SEEN BY MILLIONS. WHAT WOULD YOU WANT IT TO BE ABOUT?

IF YOU COULD ASK GOD ONE QUESTION, WHAT WOULD IT BE?

IF YOU COULD BE A PROFESSIONAL ATHLETE, WHAT SPORT WOULD YOU PLAY?

PICK ONE...AND CIRCLE IT!

- MILK SQUIRTS OUT OF YOUR EYEBALLS WHEN YOU LAUGH OR NEVER ALLOWED TO CUT YOUR HAIR?

- FAMOUS BUT NOT RICH OR RICH BUT NOT FAMOUS?

WISE WORDS:

DON'T THINK YOU ARE ALWAYS
RIGHT. BE WILLING TO LEARN
FROM OTHERS.

YOU HAVE TO BE PERMANENTLY
TRANSFORMED INTO A DISNEY®
CHARACTER—WHO DO YOU BECOME?

WHAT'S YOUR FAVORITE EXCUSE FOR NOT
GETTING YOUR HOMEWORK DONE?

WHAT DO YOU THINK HAS BEEN THE WORLD'S
GREATEST INVENTION?

IF YOU COULD BE ANY AGE, WHAT AGE WOULD YOU BE?

IF YOU HAD $1,000 TO HELP SOMEBODY,
WHAT WOULD YOU DO?

PICK THREE WORDS
THAT DESCRIBE YOU—
AND DRAW THOSE
WORDS HERE:

NAME

THIS
BOOK
GETS
AROUND

FAVORITE TV SHOW:

FAVORITE DRINK:

IF YOU WERE THE GUEST ON A POPULAR TV TALK
SHOW, WHAT WOULD YOU WANT TO TALK ABOUT?

IF YOU COULD ASK GOD ONE QUESTION,
WHAT WOULD IT BE?

THREE OF YOUR POSSESSIONS YOU COULDN'T
LIVE WITHOUT:

PICK ONE...AND CIRCLE IT!

- 3-FOOT-LONG ARMPIT HAIR THAT CAN'T BE SHAVED
  OR ALWAYS WEAR BRIGHT GREEN COWBOY BOOTS?

- PUSH AN OLD LADY OR MAKE A BABY CRY?

RETURN TO SENDER
212

DON'T FORGET...

...TO WRITE YOUR NAME ON THE CONTENTS PAGE AT THE BEGINNING OF THE BOOK, NEXT TO THE NUMBERS OF THE PAGES BELOW.

A GENIE GRANTS YOU THREE WISHES—
WHAT DO YOU WISH FOR?

WHAT PERSON DO YOU MOST ADMIRE?

IF YOU COULD GIVE THE PRESIDENT OF THE UNITED
STATES ONE PIECE OF ADVICE, WHAT WOULD IT BE?

IF YOU WERE HOSTING VISITORS FROM ANOTHER
COUNTRY, WHERE'S THE FIRST PLACE YOU
WOULD TAKE THEM?

WHAT DO YOU WANT TO BE KNOWN FOR?

YOU'RE A POET—AND
YOU KNOW IT! WRITE A
FOUR-LINE POEM ABOUT
SOCKS HERE:

NAME

THIS BOOK GETS AROUND

DON'T FORGET...

...TO WRITE YOUR NAME ON THE CONTENTS PAGE AT THE BEGINNING OF THE BOOK, NEXT TO THE NUMBERS OF THE PAGES BELOW.

FAVORITE ITEM OF CLOTHING:

FAVORITE HOBBY:

WHEN FEELING SAD, WHAT CHEERS YOU UP?

A FOOD YOU'VE NEVER TRIED, BUT WANT TO:

WHEN YOU HAVE AN HOUR OF FREE TIME,
WHAT DO YOU LIKE TO DO?

PICK ONE...AND CIRCLE IT!

- WAKE UP EARLY OR SLEEP IN?
- FOLD YOUR TP OR WAD IT UP?

IF YOU COULD ASK GOD ONE
QUESTION, WHAT WOULD IT BE?

YOU ARE KING OR QUEEN FOR A DAY. WHAT LAW
DO YOU CREATE?

ADVICE YOUR PARENTS GAVE YOU THAT YOU ACTUALLY
LISTENED TO:

A PET YOU WISH YOU HAD:

WHAT IS THE KEY TO HAPPINESS?

WISE WORDS:

THERE ARE NO
SHORTCUTS TO
ANY PLACE
WORTH GOING.

DRAW A PORTRAIT OF
YOURSELF HERE:

NAME

THIS
BOOK
GETS
AROUND

DON'T FORGET...

...TO WRITE YOUR NAME ON THE CONTENTS PAGE AT THE BEGINNING OF TH BOOK, NEXT TO THE NUMBERS OF THE PAGES BELOW.

FAVORITE BAND/SINGER OF ALL TIME:

FAVORITE AFTER-SCHOOL SNACK:

WHAT'S SOMETHING YOU'RE REALLY GOOD AT?

IF YOU COULD ASK GOD ONE QUESTION,
WHAT WOULD IT BE?

IF YOU COULD LIVE ANYWHERE IN THE WORLD,
WHERE WOULD YOU LIVE?

WRITE YOUR
FAVORITE JOKE HERE:

WISE WORDS:

WHAT YOU ARE LIKE ON THE INSIDE MATTERS MORE THAN WHAT YOU LOOK LIKE ON THE OUTSIDE.

MOST EMBARRASSING MOMENT:

WHAT SCARES YOU THE MOST?

WHO HAS HAD THE BIGGEST IMPACT ON YOUR LIFE? IN WHAT WAY?

IF YOUR LIFE WERE MADE INTO A MOVIE, WHAT WOULD THE MOVIE TITLE BE?

WHAT WORLD CAUSE OR ISSUE DO YOU CARE MOST ABOUT?

PICK ONE...AND CIRCLE IT!

- PLAY SPORTS OR READ A BOOK?
- HAVE WORLD'S SQUEAKIEST VOICE OR WORLD'S STINKIEST FEET?

NAME

THIS BOOK GETS AROUND

DON'T FORGET...

...TO WRITE YOUR NAME ON THE CONTENTS PAGE AT THE BEGINNING OF TH BOOK, NEXT TO THE NUMBERS OF THE PAGES BELOW.

FAVORITE MOVIE OF ALL TIME:

FAVORITE RADIO STATION:

SOMETHING THAT MAKES YOU LAUGH:

IF YOU COULD ASK GOD ONE QUESTION,
WHAT WOULD IT BE?

IF YOU COULD ONLY EAT ONE TYPE OF FOOD FOR THE
REST OF YOUR LIFE, WHAT WOULD IT BE?

DRAW A PICTURE OF YOUR FAVORITE ANIMAL
(USING YOUR OPPOSITE HAND!)

THE MOMENT YOU WERE MOST PROUD
OF YOURSELF:

PHYSICAL FEATURE YOU LIKE MOST ABOUT YOURSELF:

WHAT IS YOUR FAVORITE FAMILY MEMORY OR FAMILY
TRADITION?

IF YOU COULD GO BACK IN TIME,
WHAT EVENT WOULD YOU WANT TO SEE IN REAL LIFE?

WHAT DO YOU THINK ARE THE THREE MOST
IMPORTANT QUALITIES IN A FRIEND?

PICK ONE...AND CIRCLE IT!

- EAT A BOOGER OR EAT A BUG?
- SCARY MOVIES OR FUNNY MOVIES?

NAME

THIS BOOK GETS AROUND

DON'T FORGET...

...TO WRITE YOUR NAME ON THE CONTENTS PAGE AT THE BEGINNING OF TH BOOK, NEXT TO THE NUMBERS OF THE PAGES BELOW.

FAVORITE BOOK WHEN YOU WERE LITTLE:

FAVORITE SATURDAY ACTIVITY:

IF YOU HAD TO GET A TATTOO, WHAT WOULD IT BE?

IF YOU COULD ASK GOD ONE QUESTION, WHAT WOULD IT BE?

WHAT'S THE BEST VIDEO GAME YOU'VE EVER PLAYED?

PICK ONE...AND CIRCLE IT!

- GET GUM IN YOUR HAIR OR STEP IN DOG POOP WITH BARE FEET?
- GO TO PARIS WITH YOUR FAMILY OR GO CAMPING WITH YOUR FRIENDS?

THINK OUTSIDE THE BOX! USE
AS MUCH SPACE AS YOU WANT
TO DOODLE, DRAW, OR CREATE
SOMETHING FUN ON THIS PAGE!

WHAT'S SOMETHING YOU'RE REALLY GOOD AT?

WHAT DAREDEVIL STUNT WOULD YOU LIKE TO TRY?

WHAT FAMOUS PERSON WOULD YOU LIKE TO TAKE
TO A SCHOOL DANCE?

IF YOU COULD BE AN ANIMAL FOR A WEEK,
WHAT WOULD YOU BE?

IF YOU COULD DO ANYTHING YOU WANTED WITH YOUR
LIFE AND KNEW YOU WOULDN'T FAIL, WHAT WOULD
YOU DO?

WISE WORDS:

LOYALTY AND
KINDNESS ARE TWO
KEYS TO A GREAT
REPUTATION!

THIS BOOK GETS AROUND

DON'T FORGET...

...TO WRITE YOUR NAME ON THE CONTENTS PAGE AT THE BEGINNING OF TH BOOK, NEXT TO THE NUMBERS OF THE PAGES BELOW.

FAVORITE AND LEAST FAVORITE SCHOOL SUBJECTS:

FAVORITE APP:

WHAT IS THE BEST CHRISTMAS PRESENT YOU'VE EVER RECEIVED?

IF YOU COULD ASK GOD ONE QUESTION, WHAT WOULD IT BE?

YOU ARE 16 AND JUST GOT YOUR DRIVER'S LICENSE—WHAT CAR ARE YOU DRIVING AND WHERE DO YOU GO FIRST?

PICK ONE...AND CIRCLE IT!

- PASS GAS UNCONTROLLABLY OR HAVE NONSTOP BODY ODOR?
- RUN A MARATHON OR RUN FOR GOVERNOR?

DESCRIBE YOURSELF IN ONE SENTENCE:

IF THERE WERE ONLY ONE TYPE OF CANDY IN THE
WORLD, WHAT SHOULD IT BE?

A PET YOU WISH YOU HAD:

IF THE NEWSPAPER WROTE A FRONT-PAGE ARTICLE
ABOUT YOU, WHAT WOULD THE HEADLINE BE?

WHAT ARE THE THREE MOST IMPORTANT
QUALITIES IN A FRIEND?

RETURN TO SENDER
212

WITHOUT LIFTING YOUR
PEN OR PENCIL, DRAW A
MOTORCYCLE

NAME

THIS BOOK GETS AROUND

DON'T FORGET...

...TO WRITE YOUR NAME ON THE CONTENTS PAGE AT THE BEGINNING OF TH BOOK, NEXT TO THE NUMBERS OF THE PAGES BELOW.

FAVORITE WEBSITE:

TOP THREE FAVORITE SONGS:

IMAGINE MAKING A YOUTUBE® VIDEO SEEN BY MILLIONS. WHAT WOULD YOU WANT IT TO BE ABOUT?

IF YOU COULD ASK GOD ONE QUESTION, WHAT WOULD IT BE?

IF YOU COULD BE A PROFESSIONAL ATHLETE, WHAT SPORT WOULD YOU PLAY?

PICK ONE...AND CIRCLE IT!

- MILK SQUIRTS OUT OF YOUR EYEBALLS WHEN YOU LAUGH OR NEVER ALLOWED TO CUT YOUR HAIR?
- FAMOUS BUT NOT RICH OR RICH BUT NOT FAMOUS?

WISE WORDS:

DON'T THINK YOU ARE ALWAYS
RIGHT. BE WILLING TO LEARN
FROM OTHERS.

YOU HAVE TO BE PERMANENTLY
TRANSFORMED INTO A DISNEY®
CHARACTER—WHO DO YOU BECOME?

WHAT'S YOUR FAVORITE EXCUSE FOR NOT
GETTING YOUR HOMEWORK DONE?

WHAT DO YOU THINK HAS BEEN THE WORLD'S
GREATEST INVENTION?

IF YOU COULD BE ANY AGE, WHAT AGE WOULD YOU BE?

IF YOU HAD $1,000 TO HELP SOMEBODY,
WHAT WOULD YOU DO?

PICK THREE WORDS
THAT DESCRIBE YOU—
AND DRAW THOSE
WORDS HERE:

NAME

THIS
BOOK
GETS
AROUND

FAVORITE TV SHOW:

FAVORITE DRINK:

IF YOU WERE THE GUEST ON A POPULAR TV TALK
SHOW, WHAT WOULD YOU WANT TO TALK ABOUT?

IF YOU COULD ASK GOD ONE QUESTION,
WHAT WOULD IT BE?

THREE OF YOUR POSSESSIONS YOU COULDN'T
LIVE WITHOUT:

PICK ONE...AND CIRCLE IT!

- 3-FOOT-LONG ARMPIT HAIR THAT CAN'T BE SHAVED
  OR ALWAYS WEAR BRIGHT GREEN COWBOY BOOTS?
- PUSH AN OLD LADY OR MAKE A BABY CRY?

RETURN TO SENDER
212

DON'T FORGET...

...TO WRITE YOUR NAME ON THE CONTENTS PAGE AT THE BEGINNING OF THE BOOK, NEXT TO THE NUMBERS OF THE PAGES BELOW.

A GENIE GRANTS YOU THREE WISHES—
WHAT DO YOU WISH FOR?

WHAT PERSON DO YOU MOST ADMIRE?

IF YOU COULD GIVE THE PRESIDENT OF THE UNITED
STATES ONE PIECE OF ADVICE, WHAT WOULD IT BE?

IF YOU WERE HOSTING VISITORS FROM ANOTHER
COUNTRY, WHERE'S THE FIRST PLACE YOU
WOULD TAKE THEM?

WHAT DO YOU WANT TO BE KNOWN FOR?

YOU'RE A POET—AND
YOU KNOW IT! WRITE A
FOUR-LINE POEM ABOUT
SOCKS HERE:

NAME

THIS BOOK GETS AROUND

DON'T FORGET...

...TO WRITE YOUR NAME ON THE CONTENTS PAGE AT THE BEGINNING OF TH BOOK, NEXT TO THE NUMBERS OF THE PAGES BELOW.

FAVORITE ITEM OF CLOTHING:

FAVORITE HOBBY:

WHEN FEELING SAD, WHAT CHEERS YOU UP?

A FOOD YOU'VE NEVER TRIED, BUT WANT TO:

WHEN YOU HAVE AN HOUR OF FREE TIME, WHAT DO YOU LIKE TO DO?

PICK ONE...AND CIRCLE IT!

- WAKE UP EARLY OR SLEEP IN?
- FOLD YOUR TP OR WAD IT UP?

IF YOU COULD ASK GOD ONE
QUESTION, WHAT WOULD IT BE?

YOU ARE KING OR QUEEN FOR A DAY. WHAT LAW
DO YOU CREATE?

ADVICE YOUR PARENTS GAVE YOU THAT YOU ACTUALLY
LISTENED TO:

A PET YOU WISH YOU HAD:

WHAT IS THE KEY TO HAPPINESS?

DRAW A PORTRAIT OF
YOURSELF HERE:

WISE WORDS:

THERE ARE NO
SHORTCUTS TO
ANY PLACE
WORTH GOING.

35

NAME

THIS BOOK GETS AROUND

DON'T FORGET...

...TO WRITE YOUR NAME ON THE CONTENTS PAGE AT THE BEGINNING OF TH BOOK, NEXT TO THE NUMBERS OF THE PAGES BELOW.

FAVORITE BAND/SINGER OF ALL TIME:

FAVORITE AFTER-SCHOOL SNACK:

WHAT'S SOMETHING YOU'RE REALLY GOOD AT?

IF YOU COULD ASK GOD ONE QUESTION, WHAT WOULD IT BE?

IF YOU COULD LIVE ANYWHERE IN THE WORLD, WHERE WOULD YOU LIVE?

WRITE YOUR FAVORITE JOKE HERE:

MOST EMBARRASSING MOMENT:

WHAT SCARES YOU THE MOST?

WHO HAS HAD THE BIGGEST IMPACT ON YOUR LIFE? IN WHAT WAY?

IF YOUR LIFE WERE MADE INTO A MOVIE, WHAT WOULD THE MOVIE TITLE BE?

WHAT WORLD CAUSE OR ISSUE DO YOU CARE MOST ABOUT?

PICK ONE...AND CIRCLE IT!

- PLAY SPORTS OR READ A BOOK?
- HAVE WORLD'S SQUEAKIEST VOICE OR WORLD'S STINKIEST FEET?

NAME

THIS BOOK GETS AROUND

DON'T FORGET...

...TO WRITE YOUR NAME ON THE CONTENTS PAGE AT THE BEGINNING OF TH BOOK, NEXT TO THE NUMBERS OF THE PAGES BELOW.

FAVORITE MOVIE OF ALL TIME:

FAVORITE RADIO STATION:

SOMETHING THAT MAKES YOU LAUGH:

IF YOU COULD ASK GOD ONE QUESTION, WHAT WOULD IT BE?

IF YOU COULD ONLY EAT ONE TYPE OF FOOD FOR THE REST OF YOUR LIFE, WHAT WOULD IT BE?

DRAW A PICTURE OF YOUR FAVORITE ANIMAL (USING YOUR OPPOSITE HAND!)

THE MOMENT YOU WERE MOST PROUD
OF YOURSELF:

PHYSICAL FEATURE YOU LIKE MOST ABOUT YOURSELF:

WHAT IS YOUR FAVORITE FAMILY MEMORY OR FAMILY
TRADITION?

IF YOU COULD GO BACK IN TIME,
WHAT EVENT WOULD YOU WANT TO SEE IN REAL LIFE?

WHAT DO YOU THINK ARE THE THREE MOST
IMPORTANT QUALITIES IN A FRIEND?

PICK ONE...AND CIRCLE IT!

- EAT A BOOGER OR EAT A BUG?
- SCARY MOVIES OR FUNNY MOVIES?

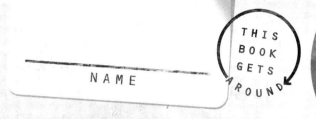

NAME

THIS BOOK GETS AROUND

DON'T FORGET...

...TO WRITE YOUR NAME ON THE CONTENTS PAGE AT THE BEGINNING OF THE BOOK, NEXT TO THE NUMBERS OF THE PAGES BELOW.

FAVORITE BOOK WHEN YOU WERE LITTLE:

FAVORITE SATURDAY ACTIVITY:

IF YOU HAD TO GET A TATTOO, WHAT WOULD IT BE?

IF YOU COULD ASK GOD ONE QUESTION, WHAT WOULD IT BE?

WHAT'S THE BEST VIDEO GAME YOU'VE EVER PLAYED?

PICK ONE...AND CIRCLE IT!

- GET GUM IN YOUR HAIR OR STEP IN DOG POOP WITH BARE FEET?

- GO TO PARIS WITH YOUR FAMILY OR GO CAMPING WITH YOUR FRIENDS?

THINK OUTSIDE THE BOX! USE
AS MUCH SPACE AS YOU WANT
TO DOODLE, DRAW, OR CREATE
SOMETHING FUN ON THIS PAGE!

WHAT'S SOMETHING YOU'RE REALLY GOOD AT?

WHAT DAREDEVIL STUNT WOULD YOU LIKE TO TRY?

WHAT FAMOUS PERSON WOULD YOU LIKE TO TAKE
TO A SCHOOL DANCE?

IF YOU COULD BE AN ANIMAL FOR A WEEK,
WHAT WOULD YOU BE?

IF YOU COULD DO ANYTHING YOU WANTED WITH YOUR
LIFE AND KNEW YOU WOULDN'T FAIL, WHAT WOULD
YOU DO?

WISE WORDS:

LOYALTY AND
KINDNESS ARE TWO
KEYS TO A GREAT
REPUTATION!

THIS BOOK GETS AROUND

DON'T FORGET...

...TO WRITE YOUR NAME ON THE CONTENTS PAGE AT THE BEGINNING OF THE BOOK, NEXT TO THE NUMBERS OF THE PAGES BELOW.

FAVORITE AND LEAST FAVORITE SCHOOL SUBJECTS:

FAVORITE APP:

WHAT IS THE BEST CHRISTMAS PRESENT YOU'VE EVER RECEIVED?

IF YOU COULD ASK GOD ONE QUESTION, WHAT WOULD IT BE?

YOU ARE 16 AND JUST GOT YOUR DRIVER'S LICENSE— WHAT CAR ARE YOU DRIVING AND WHERE DO YOU GO FIRST?

PICK ONE...AND CIRCLE IT!

- PASS GAS UNCONTROLLABLY OR HAVE NONSTOP BODY ODOR?
- RUN A MARATHON OR RUN FOR GOVERNOR?

LOYALTY AND KINDNESS ARE TWO KEYS TO A GREAT REPUTATION!

DESCRIBE YOURSELF IN ONE SENTENCE:

IF THERE WERE ONLY ONE TYPE OF CANDY IN THE WORLD, WHAT SHOULD IT BE?

A PET YOU WISH YOU HAD:

IF THE NEWSPAPER WROTE A FRONT-PAGE ARTICLE ABOUT YOU, WHAT WOULD THE HEADLINE BE?

WHAT ARE THE THREE MOST IMPORTANT QUALITIES IN A FRIEND?

RETURN TO SENDER
212

WITHOUT LIFTING YOUR PEN OR PENCIL, DRAW A MOTORCYCLE

43

NAME

THIS BOOK GETS AROUND

DON'T FORGET...

...TO WRITE YOUR NAME ON THE CONTENTS PAGE AT THE BEGINNING OF THE BOOK, NEXT TO THE NUMBERS OF THE PAGES BELOW.

FAVORITE WEBSITE:

TOP THREE FAVORITE SONGS:

IMAGINE MAKING A YOUTUBE® VIDEO SEEN BY MILLIONS. WHAT WOULD YOU WANT IT TO BE ABOUT?

IF YOU COULD ASK GOD ONE QUESTION, WHAT WOULD IT BE?

IF YOU COULD BE A PROFESSIONAL ATHLETE, WHAT SPORT WOULD YOU PLAY?

PICK ONE...AND CIRCLE IT!

- MILK SQUIRTS OUT OF YOUR EYEBALLS WHEN YOU LAUGH OR NEVER ALLOWED TO CUT YOUR HAIR?
- FAMOUS BUT NOT RICH OR RICH BUT NOT FAMOUS?

WISE WORDS:

RETURN TO SENDER
212

YOU HAVE TO BE PERMANENTLY TRANSFORMED INTO A DISNEY® CHARACTER—WHO DO YOU BECOME?

WHAT'S YOUR FAVORITE EXCUSE FOR NOT GETTING YOUR HOMEWORK DONE?

WHAT DO YOU THINK HAS BEEN THE WORLD'S GREATEST INVENTION?

IF YOU COULD BE ANY AGE, WHAT AGE WOULD YOU BE?

IF YOU HAD $1,000 TO HELP SOMEBODY, WHAT WOULD YOU DO?

PICK THREE WORDS THAT DESCRIBE YOU— AND DRAW THOSE WORDS HERE:

4

NAME _____

WISE WORDS:

CHOOSE YOUR
FRIENDS WISELY—
YOU BECOME LIKE
THE PEOPLE YOU
SPEND TIME WITH.

FAVORITE TV SHOW:

FAVORITE DRINK:

IF YOU WERE THE GUEST ON A POPULAR TV TALK
SHOW, WHAT WOULD YOU WANT TO TALK ABOUT?

IF YOU COULD ASK GOD ONE QUESTION,
WHAT WOULD IT BE?

THREE OF YOUR POSSESSIONS YOU COULDN'T
LIVE WITHOUT:

PICK ONE...AND CIRCLE IT!

- 3-FOOT-LONG ARMPIT HAIR THAT CAN'T BE SHAVED
  OR ALWAYS WEAR BRIGHT GREEN COWBOY BOOTS?
- PUSH AN OLD LADY OR MAKE A BABY CRY?

RETURN TO SENDER
212

DON'T FORGET...

...TO WRITE YOUR NAME ON THE CONTENTS PAGE AT THE BEGINNING OF THE BOOK, NEXT TO THE NUMBERS OF THE PAGES BELOW.

A GENIE GRANTS YOU THREE WISHES— WHAT DO YOU WISH FOR?

WHAT PERSON DO YOU MOST ADMIRE?

IF YOU COULD GIVE THE PRESIDENT OF THE UNITED STATES ONE PIECE OF ADVICE, WHAT WOULD IT BE?

IF YOU WERE HOSTING VISITORS FROM ANOTHER COUNTRY, WHERE'S THE FIRST PLACE YOU WOULD TAKE THEM?

WHAT DO YOU WANT TO BE KNOWN FOR?

YOU'RE A POET—AND YOU KNOW IT! WRITE A FOUR-LINE POEM ABOUT SOCKS HERE:

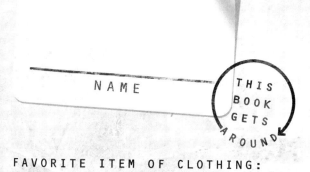

NAME

DON'T FORGET...

...TO WRITE YOUR NAME ON THE CONTENTS PAGE AT THE BEGINNING OF TH BOOK, NEXT TO THE NUMBERS OF THE PAGES BELOW.

FAVORITE ITEM OF CLOTHING:

FAVORITE HOBBY:

WHEN FEELING SAD, WHAT CHEERS YOU UP?

A FOOD YOU'VE NEVER TRIED, BUT WANT TO:

WHEN YOU HAVE AN HOUR OF FREE TIME, WHAT DO YOU LIKE TO DO?

PICK ONE...AND CIRCLE IT!

- WAKE UP EARLY OR SLEEP IN?
- FOLD YOUR TP OR WAD IT UP?

RETURN TO SENDER
212

IF YOU COULD ASK GOD ONE
QUESTION, WHAT WOULD IT BE?

YOU ARE KING OR QUEEN FOR A DAY. WHAT LAW
DO YOU CREATE?

ADVICE YOUR PARENTS GAVE YOU THAT YOU ACTUALLY
LISTENED TO:

A PET YOU WISH YOU HAD:

WHAT IS THE KEY TO HAPPINESS?

DRAW A PORTRAIT OF
YOURSELF HERE:

WISE WORDS:

THERE ARE NO
SHORTCUTS TO
ANY PLACE
WORTH GOING.

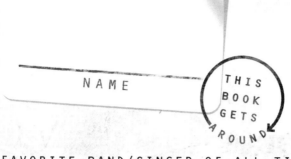

NAME

THIS BOOK GETS AROUND

DON'T FORGET...

...TO WRITE YOUR NAME ON THE CONTENTS PAGE AT THE BEGINNING OF TH BOOK, NEXT TO THE NUMBERS OF THE PAGES BELOW.

FAVORITE BAND/SINGER OF ALL TIME:

FAVORITE AFTER-SCHOOL SNACK:

WHAT'S SOMETHING YOU'RE REALLY GOOD AT?

IF YOU COULD ASK GOD ONE QUESTION, WHAT WOULD IT BE?

IF YOU COULD LIVE ANYWHERE IN THE WORLD, WHERE WOULD YOU LIVE?

WRITE YOUR FAVORITE JOKE HERE:

MOST EMBARRASSING MOMENT:

WHAT SCARES YOU THE MOST?

WHO HAS HAD THE BIGGEST IMPACT ON YOUR LIFE? IN WHAT WAY?

IF YOUR LIFE WERE MADE INTO A MOVIE, WHAT WOULD THE MOVIE TITLE BE?

WHAT WORLD CAUSE OR ISSUE DO YOU CARE MOST ABOUT?

PICK ONE...AND CIRCLE IT!

- PLAY SPORTS OR READ A BOOK?
- HAVE WORLD'S SQUEAKIEST VOICE OR WORLD'S STINKIEST FEET?

NAME

THIS BOOK GETS AROUND

DON'T FORGET...

...TO WRITE YOUR NAME ON THE CONTENTS PAGE AT THE BEGINNING OF THE BOOK, NEXT TO THE NUMBERS OF THE PAGES BELOW.

FAVORITE MOVIE OF ALL TIME:

FAVORITE RADIO STATION:

SOMETHING THAT MAKES YOU LAUGH:

IF YOU COULD ASK GOD ONE QUESTION,
WHAT WOULD IT BE?

IF YOU COULD ONLY EAT ONE TYPE OF FOOD FOR THE
REST OF YOUR LIFE, WHAT WOULD IT BE?

DRAW A PICTURE OF YOUR FAVORITE ANIMAL
(USING YOUR OPPOSITE HAND!)

WISE WORDS:

LOYALTY AND KINDNESS ARE TWO KEYS TO A GREAT REPUTATION!

THE MOMENT YOU WERE MOST PROUD OF YOURSELF:

PHYSICAL FEATURE YOU LIKE MOST ABOUT YOURSELF:

WHAT IS YOUR FAVORITE FAMILY MEMORY OR FAMILY TRADITION?

IF YOU COULD GO BACK IN TIME, WHAT EVENT WOULD YOU WANT TO SEE IN REAL LIFE?

WHAT DO YOU THINK ARE THE THREE MOST IMPORTANT QUALITIES IN A FRIEND?

PICK ONE...AND CIRCLE IT!

- EAT A BOOGER OR EAT A BUG?
- SCARY MOVIES OR FUNNY MOVIES?

NAME _____

THIS
BOOK
GETS
AROUND

DON'T FORGET...

...TO WRITE YOUR
NAME ON THE
CONTENTS PAGE AT
THE BEGINNING OF TH
BOOK, NEXT TO THE
NUMBERS OF THE
PAGES BELOW.

FAVORITE BOOK WHEN YOU WERE LITTLE:

FAVORITE SATURDAY ACTIVITY:

IF YOU HAD TO GET A TATTOO, WHAT WOULD IT BE?

IF YOU COULD ASK GOD ONE QUESTION,
WHAT WOULD IT BE?

WHAT'S THE BEST VIDEO GAME YOU'VE EVER PLAYED?

PICK ONE...AND CIRCLE IT!

- GET GUM IN YOUR HAIR OR
  STEP IN DOG POOP WITH BARE FEET?
- GO TO PARIS WITH YOUR FAMILY OR
  GO CAMPING WITH YOUR FRIENDS?

THINK OUTSIDE THE BOX! USE
AS MUCH SPACE AS YOU WANT
TO DOODLE, DRAW, OR CREATE
SOMETHING FUN ON THIS PAGE!

WHAT'S SOMETHING YOU'RE REALLY GOOD AT?

WHAT DAREDEVIL STUNT WOULD YOU LIKE TO TRY?

WHAT FAMOUS PERSON WOULD YOU LIKE TO TAKE
TO A SCHOOL DANCE?

IF YOU COULD BE AN ANIMAL FOR A WEEK,
WHAT WOULD YOU BE?

IF YOU COULD DO ANYTHING YOU WANTED WITH YOUR
LIFE AND KNEW YOU WOULDN'T FAIL, WHAT WOULD
YOU DO?

WISE WORDS:

LOYALTY AND
KINDNESS ARE TWO
KEYS TO A GREAT
REPUTATION!